All New Very Easy
TRUE STORIES

A PICTURE-BASED FIRST READER

by Sandra Heyer

PEARSON
Longman

For Myrna, who listens to everyone's stories.

All New Very Easy True Stories: A Picture-Based First Reader

Copyright © 2006 by Pearson Education, Inc.
All rights reserved.
No part of this publication may be reproduced, stored in a retrieval system, or transmitted in any form or by any means, electronic, mechanical, photocopying, recording, or otherwise, without the prior permission of the publisher.

Pearson Education, 10 Bank Street, White Plains, NY 10606

Staff credits: The people who made up the *All New Very Easy True Stories* team, representing editorial, production, design, and manufacturing, are: Elizabeth Carlson, Dana Klinek, Laura Lazzaretti, Laura Le Dréan, Melissa Leyva, and Edith Pullman.

Cover design: Elizabeth Carlson
Text composition: Integra Software Graphics
Text font: 12/14 Palatino
Text art: Don Martinetti and Andrés Morales
Text credits: See page 91.
Photo credits: See page 92.

Library of Congress Cataloging-in-Publication Data

Heyer, Sandra.
   All new very easy true stories: a picture-based first reader / by Sandra Heyer.
      p.   cm.
   ISBN 0-13-134556-7
   1. English language—Textbooks for foreign speakers.   2. Readers.
   I. Title.
   PE1128.H435463 2006
   428.6'4—dc22

                                                                        2005018818

ISBN: 0-13-134556-7

Printed in the United States of America
9 10 11 12 13 14 15—CRS—15 14 13 12 11 10

Contents

Introduction

All New Very Easy True Stories is a first reader for students of English. It is for absolute beginners who are familiar with the Roman alphabet and have some experience reading words and sentences, as well as for students with well-developed speaking and listening skills but low-level literacy skills. It is a companion book to *Very Easy True Stories*; that is, it is written at the same reading level and has the same format. However, as the title indicates, it has all new stories and exercises.

PURPOSE

Why does the *True Stories* series offer two first readers? First, some students need more time at the introductory level before moving on to *Easy True Stories* and *All New Easy True Stories*, the next books in the series. This is particularly true for students with only basic literacy skills in their native languages. *All New Very Easy True Stories* gives students the option of lingering a while at this level. They can go back and forth between *Very Easy True Stories* and *All New Very Easy True Stories*, or they can complete first one book and then the other. (Students can read either book first.) Second, many teachers like to incorporate reading into their thematically based instructional units. The story "The Parking Ticket," for example, adds dimension to a unit on traffic signs, and "Wrong Number" complements a unit on phone etiquette. With 28 low-level stories, teachers have multiple opportunities to match readings with other classroom activities. Third, a choice of two books helps veteran teachers keep their lessons fresh: They can use *Very Easy True Stories* one semester and *All New Very Easy True Stories* the next. Alternating between the two books also keeps the lessons fresh for students who choose to stay in an introductory class when their classmates move on to the next level. They can essentially repeat the class but with all new material.

Very Easy True Stories and *All New Very Easy True Stories* can also be used in higher-level classes as the basis of a cooperative reading/speaking/listening activity. One group of students reads a story in one book while another group reads a story in the other book. Then, in pairs, students from one group tell their story to students from the other group, using the drawings as cues as they retell the story.

DESCRIPTION

All New Very Easy True Stories contains 14 units, each centered on a story that was adapted from a newspaper article and written in the simplest, most concrete language possible. In answer to those students who think that some stories are too amazing to be true: Yes, the stories are true, to the best of our knowledge. The two girls really did use a blanket to catch the boy who fell from a window, and customers waiting in line at a store really did chip in to buy the toy for the woman who had lost her money. In the back of the book, you will find a special To the Teacher section with more information about each story.

HOW TO USE *ALL NEW VERY EASY TRUE STORIES*

Each unit is divided into three sections: pre-reading, reading, and post-reading exercises. Following are some suggestions for using each of the sections. Teachers new to the field might find these suggestions especially helpful. Please keep in mind that these are only suggestions. Teachers should, of course, feel free to adapt these strategies to best suit their teaching styles and their students' learning styles.

PRE-READING

You might want to introduce each unit by acquainting (or reacquainting) students with key words in the story. Most of the nouns in the stories are concrete objects (*vegetables*, *house*, *car*), and most of the verbs are simple actions (*sit*, *swim*, *drive*), so you can easily clarify meaning by drawing pictures, by showing photos or realia, or by acting out words. (If students have difficulty differentiating between common and proper nouns, treat the names of people in the stories as new vocabulary. Draw a simple figure on the board, write the person's name beneath it, and say, for example, "His name is Genesio.") When you are satisfied that students know the key words, proceed to the pre-reading drawing, which introduces the theme of the story and prompts students to recall knowledge and experiences related to the theme. Here is one possible sequence of steps for using the pre-reading drawing.

1. With the help of the pre-reading drawing, elicit the vocabulary of the story.

Ask students to turn to the pre-reading drawing in their books. (Or make a transparency of the pre-reading page, and show it on the overhead projector.) Ask students, "What do you see?" Write their responses on the board, on flashcards, or directly on the transparency. (Some teachers advocate printing in block letters, rather than in upper- and lowercase letters, since block printing is easier for students to copy.) As you write, say the words slowly to model correct pronunciation. Students copy the words onto the picture in their books.

If all the students are absolute beginners, it is unlikely they will be able to supply the vocabulary for the pre-reading drawing. Instead of asking students, "What do you see?" begin by simply labeling the items and actions depicted in the drawing and slowly pronouncing the words. Say only five or six words. That's plenty for beginners. Resist the inclination to talk to yourself as you label ("Let's see . . . and over here there's a . . .").

2. Tell students what the story is about.

Point to the title of the story, and read it aloud slowly. Then connect the vocabulary of the pre-reading drawing to the title. For example, say, "This story is about a custodian." (Point to the man in the drawing.) "His name is Genesio." (Point to the word "Genesio" in the title.) As students progress through the book, try to stop at "This story is about . . ." and see if students can use the pre-reading drawing and the title of the story to make predictions about the story.

Teaching Absolute Beginners

All New Very Easy True Stories was field-tested in several ESL environments. One of those environments was a class of zero-level adult learners, all native speakers of Spanish. Before beginning Unit 1, the teacher told his students—in Spanish—that they were going to hear and read a story. He told his students not to worry about understanding every word, but to try to get the gist of the story. He said that in the course of reading the story, maybe they'd learn a couple of new words, and that would be great! Those few words in Spanish instantly changed the atmosphere in the classroom: The students went from looking apprehensive to looking relaxed. Their goal had changed from the impossible to the possible—instead of trying to understand every word, they were just going to enjoy the story and maybe pick up a few new words (a goal they did, in fact, accomplish).

If you have absolute beginners in your class, it is well worth the effort to find people—more advanced students in the same class, perhaps, or in another class in your program—to make a similar announcement in your students' native languages. When you do find native speakers to make the announcement, consider asking them to write it down for you so you'll be able to encourage future students in their native languages.

READING

Following is one possible sequence of steps in reading the story:

1. Read the story aloud to the students.

Ask students to turn to the second and third pages of the unit, which are in comic-strip format. (Or make transparencies of these pages and show them on the overhead projector.) Tell students to look at just the drawings for now, not at the words beneath the drawings. The purpose of this first reading is to give students a global, not a word-for-word, understanding of the story.

Read the story aloud as students look at the drawings. Begin by saying "Number one," and slowly read the sentences that the first drawing illustrates. Then say "Number two," and read the appropriate sentences. Continue in this manner. Saying the numbers of the pictures while telling the story ensures that all eyes are on the same picture.

If your students are absolute beginners, you might need to reduce the story to its most basic elements when you tell it the first time. In Unit 1, for example, instead of reading the story exactly as it is written ("He doesn't buy new clothes. He wears old clothes"), you might say, "New clothes? No! Old clothes? Yes!"

You will probably want to walk away from the pictures from time to time and act out some scenes, perhaps with the help of props, or you might want to act out the entire story if it has plenty of action. (The teacher who field-tested "An Expensive Vacation" came to class with a ski jacket, a lighter, a few pieces of wood, and bills in $1, $5, $10, and $20 denominations. By the time the teacher "burned" the ten-dollar bills, all eyes were riveted on the scene.)

Some of the stories build suspense. You might stop short of the last few sentences when reading those stories aloud and let students—silently—read how the story ends.

2. Read the story a second time.

This time, however, instruct students to look at the words beneath the pictures. During subsequent readings, you might wish to call students' attention to basic grammatical structures, not by giving lengthy explanations, but by reminding students of rules they have already learned. (For example, after reading the sentence "He goes to free concerts in the park," say, "I go, you go, they go, we go, she goes, he goes.")

3. Give students time to read the story silently.

Some students will be ready to go to the fourth page and read the story in text form. Other students will need to read the story in comic-strip format so that they can go back and forth between the words and the pictures to check their understanding.

4. Present the story in a different way.

If students have a global understanding of the story but need practice mastering its language, you might try one of these activities:

• Read the story aloud, but this time make "mistakes." ("Genesio is a mechanic. He works at a garage. He cleans the cars.") Pause after each sentence, letting students speak in chorus to correct the mistake, rather than calling on individuals. A variation of this technique is to make mistakes in only *some* of the sentences. Students say "Yes" if the sentence is correct, "No" if it isn't. (Some teachers like to give each student two differently colored index cards. On one card "YES" is printed; on the other card "NO" is printed. After hearing each sentence, students hold up the card with their answers.)
• Read the story aloud, sentence by sentence, and ask the entire class to repeat, echoing your pronunciation, intonation, and rhythm.
• Read sentences from the story at random. Students call out the number of the corresponding picture.
• Say key words in the story. Students scan to find the words and circle them; they can verify their work by checking with a partner.

Teaching Young Students

If you teach young students, you may need to use one of the four activities above instead of, not in addition to, having students read the story on their own. Adults understand that looking at the pictures while hearing the story is a helpful pre-reading step; children see it as an end unto itself. Middle school students who participated in field-testing material were somewhat puzzled by the teacher's request that they read the story silently. They had just heard the story, and they knew how it ended. Why would they want to *read* it? When, however, reading the story was made into a game, they were enthusiastic readers. They especially liked identifying mistakes in the teacher's version of the story and scanning for key words (an activity that they turned into a race to see who could find the words first).

THE POST-READING EXERCISES

Pronunciation

The exercise section begins with an activity that helps students correlate English letters with the sounds they represent. Some units focus on vowel sounds, others on consonant sounds. In the course of the book, the pronunciation activity acquaints students with 12 vowel sounds and 16 consonant sounds. Exercises that highlight vowel sounds group words in the story according to their accented vowel sound. Students, especially those whose first language is phonetic, are usually surprised to discover that the five English vowels make more than 5 sounds. The purpose of the exercise is simply to make students aware that these sounds exist in English, not to drill students into pronouncing the sounds perfectly. (In fact, doing so would probably be a disservice. Keep in mind that some vowels make one sound when they are stressed, as they are in the exercise, but change to the neutral vowel [∂] when they are in an unstressed position. Consider how the pronunciation of the *a* in *and* changes when *and* is put in an unstressed position: *cream and sugar.*)

If your students have high-level speaking skills, you might pause after each column of words and ask, "Do you know other words with this sound?" Write their contributions on the board.

Spelling

This exercise is a dictation exercise. For absolute beginners, write the words on the board so that they can copy them. More advanced students like to work this exercise like a puzzle, trying to figure out the word from the letters given and announcing it before the teacher can say it.

Comprehension

Students can complete these exercises individually, in pairs, in small groups, or as a whole class. The exercises can be completed in class or assigned as homework. At the back of the book there is an answer key to the exercises. Note that many of the exercises not only test comprehension but subtly call students' attention to English syntax. For example, an exercise that asks students to match the first half of a compound sentence ("Ann steps on the brake") with the second half ("and her car goes faster") also makes students aware that the word *and* often connects two parts of a compound sentence.

Speaking and Writing

These exercises personalize the themes of the stories. They are written at a level parallel to that of the readings; that is, they assume that students speak and write about as well as they read. As a result, these exercises rarely introduce new vocabulary; the vocabulary consists of words recycled from the story. If, however, your students are fairly proficient speakers, you will probably want to encourage them to talk about the stories, asking them, for example, if they, like Ann, have ever had trouble with a car's brakes, or if they, like Ken Walker, have ever gotten help from someone on the Internet.

You could let the discussion lead into a writing activity, using the Language Experience Approach. Briefly, the Language Experience Approach consists of these steps:

1. The student orally relates a story or experience.
2. The teacher writes the student's words (sitting next to the student so the student can see what is being written).
3. The teacher reads the story.
4. The student reads the story.

Keep in mind that the first step in the Language Experience Approach is an oral one. If your students are zero-level speakers of English, you will not want to venture from the controlled speaking exercises in the book.

Students in a beginning ESL class can have a wide range of experience with English, as you may know only too well. Some students may be at zero level in all the skills areas—reading, writing, speaking, and listening. Other students may have well-developed speaking and listening skills but low-level literacy skills. Another group may have studied English in their native countries, perhaps for years, and be fairly proficient readers and writers; but they may have been placed in a beginning class because they are unable to speak or understand spoken English. So, you may have to tinker with the exercises—to adjust them up or down, to skip some, or to add some of your own.

Both the exercises and reading selections are intended to build students' confidence along with their reading skills. Above all, it is hoped that reading *All New Very Easy True Stories* will be a pleasure, for both you and your students.

All New Very Easy True Stories and *Very Easy True Stories* are the first books in the *True Stories* reading series. They are followed by *Easy True Stories, All New Easy True Stories, True Stories in the News, More True Stories, Even More True Stories,* and *Beyond True Stories.*

Genesio's Gift

1. PRE-READING

- Look at the picture. What do you see?
- Say the words.
- Watch your teacher write the words.
- Copy the words onto the picture.

2. READING

- Listen to your teacher read the story. Look at the pictures.
- Listen to your teacher read the story again. Look at the words.

Genesio Morlacci is a custodian.

He works at a university.

He cleans the classrooms.

Genesio makes money,

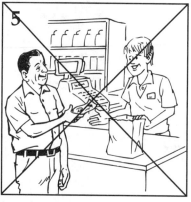

but he doesn't like to spend it.

He doesn't buy new clothes.

He wears old clothes.

He doesn't buy vegetables.

He has a garden.

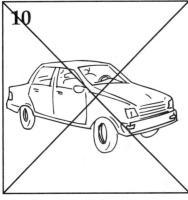

10

He doesn't drive a big car.

11

He drives a small car.

12

He doesn't live in a big house.

13

He lives in a small house.

14

TICKETS

He doesn't go to movies.

15

He goes to free concerts in the park.

16

Genesio
Morlacci

1902 – 2004

Genesio dies when he is 102 years old.

17

He gives all his money to the university. The money is for the students.

18

GENESIO MORLACCI
4015483380
UNITED STATES OF AMERICA   Date: Nov. 22, 2004

Pay to the order of: University of Great Falls $ 2,300,000.00

Amount: Two million three hundred thousand and 00/100

WFB WESTERN FINANCIAL BANK   Signature

0231 511800210 04015493380 9255293
                COUNT NUMBER   CHECK NUMBER

How much money does Genesio give? He gives 2.3 million dollars.[1]

---

[1] $2,300,000.00

• Read the story again.

Genesio's Gift

Genesio Morlacci is a custodian. He works at a university. He cleans the classrooms.

Genesio makes money, but he doesn't like to spend it. He doesn't buy new clothes. He wears old clothes. He doesn't buy vegetables. He has a garden. He doesn't drive a big car. He drives a small car. He doesn't live in a big house. He lives in a small house. He doesn't go to movies. He goes to free concerts in the park.

Genesio dies when he is 102 years old. He gives all his money to the university. The money is for the students.

How much money does Genesio give? He gives 2.3 million dollars.[1]

---

[1] $2,300,000.00

3. PRONUNCIATION

What are the letters? What sounds can they make? Listen to your teacher.
Say the words.

s
spend
small
house
works
makes
students

s
has
lives
gives
buys
movies
dollars

c / k
car
clean
class
park
work
like

m
make
money
much
million
movie

4. VOCABULARY

Which words go together? Write your answer on the line.

money	clothes	a car
in a house	to a concert	

1. drive   _a car_

2. live   _____

3. wear   _____

4. spend   _____

5. go   _____

5. COMPREHENSION

What does Genesio do? Check (✔) five answers. The first one is done for you.

He . . .

☑ drives a small car.   ☐ wears old clothes.

☐ buys new clothes.   ☐ drives a big car.

☐ goes to movies.   ☐ lives in a small house.

☐ has a garden.   ☐ buys vegetables.

☐ lives in a big house.   ☐ goes to free concerts in the park.

6. SPEAKING

Draw a picture on your own paper. In the picture, you are doing something you like to do. But you are not spending money (or only a little money). Under your picture write what you are doing. Then share your picture with the class. For example:

I am listening to music.

7. WRITING

Write the sentences correctly.

1. Genesioisacustodian.

    Genesio is a custodian.

2. Hecleanstheclassroomsatauniversity.

    _____

3. Hemakesmoney,buthedoesn'tliketospendit.

    _____

4. Hedieswhenheis102yearsold.

    _____

5. Hegives2.3milliondollarstotheuniversity.

    _____

The Surprise

1. PRE-READING

- Look at the picture. What do you see?
- Say the words.
- Watch your teacher write the words.
- Copy the words onto the picture.

2. READING

- Listen to your teacher read the story. Look at the pictures.
- Listen to your teacher read the story again. Look at the words.

Amy is sad.

She has a boyfriend. His name is Ian.

Ian is far away.

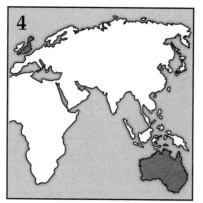

He is working in Australia, and Amy lives in England.

She misses him.

Amy wants to see Ian.

She buys a plane ticket to Australia.

She is going to visit Ian, but she doesn't tell him.

It is a surprise.

Ian is sad, too. He misses Amy.

He wants to see her.

He buys a plane ticket to England.

He is going to visit Amy, but he doesn't tell her.

It is a surprise.

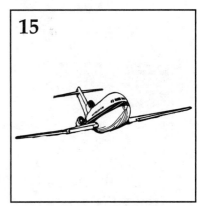

Ian flies to England.

He goes to Amy's apartment. She is not there. Where is she?

She is at Ian's apartment in Australia.

What a surprise for Amy! What a surprise for Ian!

- Read the story again.

The Surprise

Amy is sad. She has a boyfriend. His name is Ian. Ian is far away. He is working in Australia, and Amy lives in England. She misses him.

Amy wants to see Ian. She buys a plane ticket to Australia. She is going to visit Ian, but she doesn't tell him. It is a surprise.

Ian is sad, too. He misses Amy. He wants to see her. He buys a plane ticket to England. He is going to visit Amy, but he doesn't tell her. It is a surprise.

Ian flies to England. He goes to Amy's apartment. She is not there. Where is she? She is at Ian's apartment in Australia. What a surprise for Amy! What a surprise for Ian!

3. PRONUNCIATION

What are the letters? What sounds can they make? Listen to your teacher. Say the words.

i
is
in
it
him

a
at
and
sad

a / u
a
what
but

a / o
want
not

e / ee
she
he
see

4. SPELLING

Listen to your teacher say the words. Write the missing letters. Then copy the words.

1. bo _y_ fri _e_ nd   _boyfriend_

2. f ___ r   _____

3. mi ___ s   _____

4. t ___ ll   _____

5. b ___ y   _____

6. ___ lan ___   _____

5. VOCABULARY

What do you see in the pictures? Write the words on the lines.

far away   ~~plane ticket~~   Australia   surprise   England

1. _plane ticket_   2. _____   3. _____

4. _____   5. _____

6. COMPREHENSION

Which sentence is correct? Circle a or b.

1. **a.** Amy is happy.
   b. Amy is sad.

2. **a.** Her brother, Ian, is far away.
   b. Her boyfriend, Ian, is far away.

3. **a.** Ian is working in Australia.
   b. Ian is on vacation in Australia.

4. **a.** Ian drives to England.
   b. Ian flies to England.

5. **a.** Ian sees Amy in England.
   b. Ian doesn't see Amy in England.

6. **a.** It is a bad surprise.
   b. It is a good surprise.

7. SPEAKING

Ian misses Amy, and Amy misses Ian. Do you miss someone or something?

Tell your teacher what you miss. Your teacher will write your name and your answer on the board. For example:

Ornela	my mother's cooking
Mirna	my brother
Jorge	the busy life in my city

8. WRITING

On you own paper, write five sentences with the information on the board. For example:

Ornela misses her mother's cooking.

Mirna misses her brother.

Jorge misses the busy life in his city.

Hiccup! Hiccup!

1. PRE-READING

- Look at the picture. What do you see?
- Say the words.
- Watch your teacher write the words.
- Copy the words onto the picture.

2. READING

- Listen to your teacher read the story. Look at the pictures.
- Listen to your teacher read the story again. Look at the words.

Charles is 28 years old. He is a farmer.

One day Charles lifts a big pig and puts it on a truck.

Then he starts to hiccup. He hiccups, and hiccups, and hiccups. He can't stop.

"Drink a glass of water," his wife says.

Charles drinks a glass of water. The hiccups don't stop.

"Eat some sugar," his mother says.

Charles eats some sugar. The hiccups don't stop.

"Eat some lemon," his father says.

Charles eats some lemon. The hiccups don't stop.

10

"Close your mouth and hold your nose," his sister says.

11

Charles closes his mouth and holds his nose. The hiccups don't stop.

12

"Pull your tongue," his grandfather says.

13

Charles pulls his tongue. The hiccups don't stop.

14

"Put water in your mouth," his grandmother says. "Then put your fingers in your ears and swallow the water."

15

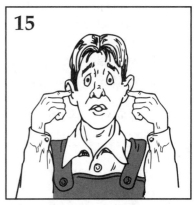

Charles puts water in his mouth. Then he puts his fingers in his ears and swallows the water. The hiccups don't stop.

16

Charles hiccups for 68 years, from 1922 to 1990.

17

Then one day the hiccups suddenly stop.

18

Charles is a happy old man. Finally, he doesn't have the hiccups!

- Read the story again.

Hiccup! Hiccup!

Charles is 28 years old. He is a farmer. One day Charles lifts a big pig and puts it on a truck. Then he starts to hiccup. He hiccups, and hiccups, and hiccups. He can't stop.

"Drink a glass of water," his wife says. Charles drinks a glass of water. The hiccups don't stop.

"Eat some sugar," his mother says. Charles eats some sugar. The hiccups don't stop.

"Eat some lemon," his father says. Charles eats some lemon. The hiccups don't stop.

"Close your mouth and hold your nose," his sister says. Charles closes his mouth and holds his nose. The hiccups don't stop.

"Pull your tongue," his grandfather says. Charles pulls his tongue. The hiccups don't stop.

"Put water in your mouth," his grandmother says. "Then put your fingers in your ears and swallow the water." Charles puts water in his mouth. Then he puts his fingers in his ears and swallows the water. The hiccups don't stop.

Charles hiccups for 68 years, from 1922 to 1990. Then one day the hiccups suddenly stop. Charles is a happy old man. Finally, he doesn't have the hiccups!

3. PRONUNCIATION

Listen to your teacher. Say the words.

s	
drink	drinks
eat	eats
put	puts

s	
pull	pulls
swallow	swallows
close	closes

4. VOCABULARY

What do you see in the pictures? Write the words on the lines.

farmer   pull   lift   ~~tongue~~   mouth   fingers

1. _tongue_   2. _____ 3. _____

4. _____   5. _____ 6. _____

5. COMPREHENSION

Complete the sentences.

One day Charles lifts a pig. Then he starts to ———————————.

1
He can't stop. He drinks a ——————————— of water. He eats

2
some ——————————— and some lemon. He closes his mouth and

3
——————————— his nose. He pulls his tongue. He puts water in

4
his mouth. Then he puts his fingers in his ears and ———————————

5
the water. The hiccups don't stop.

Charles hiccups for ——————————— years. Then one day the

6
hiccups suddenly stop. Charles is a ——————————— old man.

7

6. SPEAKING

A. How do you stop the hiccups? Tell or show the class.

B. Say the sentences and act them out.[1]

1. Lift a pig.
2. Drink a glass of water.
3. Eat a lemon.
4. Close your mouth and hold your nose.
5. Put your fingers in your ears.
6. Swallow.

7. WRITING

Your teacher will say the sentences in Exercise 6 (in any order). Listen to each sentence. Then copy it on your own paper.

---

[1] The directions for this activity are on page 86.

Wrong Number

1. PRE-READING

- Look at the picture. What do you see?
- Say the words.
- Watch your teacher write the words.
- Copy the words onto the picture.

2. READING

- Listen to your teacher read the story. Look at the pictures.
- Listen to your teacher read the story again. Look at the words.

It is nine o'clock in the evening.

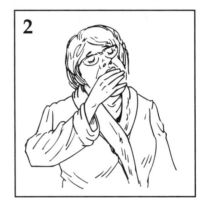

Mary is tired.

She goes into the living room and sits down in her favorite chair. "Ah," she says.

The phone rings in the kitchen.

Mary gets up, goes into the kitchen, and answers the phone. "Hello," she says.

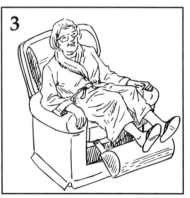

"Is Jeff there?" a young woman asks.

"There's no Jeff here," Mary says.

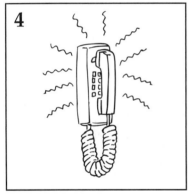

"Is this 555-4132?" the woman asks.

"No, you have the wrong number," Mary says. "Sorry," the woman says.

10

BOOM! A truck crashes into Mary's house.

11

The living room wall falls down.

12

It falls on Mary's chair.

13

Mary goes back into the living room.

14

She is shocked.

15

But she is happy, too.

16

She is not happy about the wall.

17

She is not happy about her favorite chair.

18

But she *is* happy about the wrong number!

Wrong Number

It is nine o'clock in the evening. Mary is tired. She goes into the living room and sits down in her favorite chair. "Ah," she says.

The phone rings in the kitchen. Mary gets up, goes into the kitchen, and answers the phone. "Hello," she says.

"Is Jeff there?" a young woman asks.

"There's no Jeff here," Mary says.

"Is this 555-4132?" the woman asks.

"No, you have the wrong number," Mary says.

"Sorry," the woman says.

BOOM! A truck crashes into Mary's house. The living room wall falls down. It falls on Mary's chair.

Mary goes back into the living room. She is shocked. But she is happy, too. She is not happy about the wall. She is not happy about her favorite chair. But she *is* happy about the wrong number!

3. PRONUNCIATION

In the United States and Canada, people write phone numbers this way: 555-4132. They say phone numbers this way, in three parts: 555 41 32.

Listen to your teacher. Say the phone numbers.

555-4132	592-7413	819-0168
471-6908	296-8324	673-5037

4. VOCABULARY

What do you see in the pictures? Write the words on the lines.

evening
~~wall~~

answer the phone
wrong number

crash
shocked

1. _wall_

2. _____

3. _____

4. _____

5. _____

6. _____

5. COMPREHENSION

Complete the sentences. Circle a or b.

1. Mary is
   a. sad.
   b. tired.

2. She goes into the living room and sits down
   a. on the sofa.
   b. in her favorite chair.

3. The phone rings
   a. in the kitchen.
   b. in the living room.

4. A young woman asks,
   a. "How are you?"
   b. "Is this 555-4132?"

5. Mary says,
   a. "You have the wrong number."
   b. "I'm fine. How are you?"

6. A truck hits
   a. Mary's house.
   b. a tree.

7. The living room wall falls on
   a. Mary's chair.
   b. Mary.

8. Mary is
   a. shocked.
   b. angry.

6. SPEAKING

Sit with a partner and read the conversation aloud. Student A begins.

Student A	Student B
1. Hello.	Hi. Is Jeff there?
2. There's no Jeff here.	Is this 555-4132?
3. No, it isn't. You have the wrong number.	Oh. Sorry.
4. No problem.	

7. WRITING

Copy the correct answers in Exercise 5 on your own paper. For example:

Mary is tired. She goes into . . .

The Catch

1. PRE-READING

- Look at the picture. What do you see?
- Say the words.
- Watch your teacher write the words.
- Copy the words onto the picture.

2. READING

- Listen to your teacher read the story. Look at the pictures.
- Listen to your teacher read the story again. Look at the words.

1

Stephanie and Samantha are friends. Stephanie is nine years old, and Samantha is six.

2

They are sitting outside on a blanket.

3

The girls are sitting next to a big apartment building.

4

They look up.

5

A little boy is crawling out a window.

6

It is on the fourth floor.

7

Stephanie and Samantha pick up the blanket

8

and run to the building.

9

They hold the blanket under the window.

10

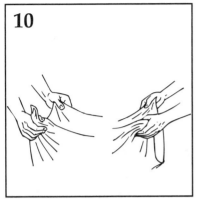

Stephanie holds one side of the blanket, and Samantha holds the other side.

11

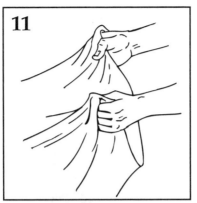

"Hold on tight," Stephanie tells Samantha.

12

The boy's head, shoulders, and arms are out the window.

13

He puts his leg out the window.

14

Then he falls.

15

Stephanie and Samantha catch him in the blanket.

16

Paramedics come.

17

The boy is fine. "Lucky boy," the paramedics say.

18

"Smart girls."

• Read the story again.

The Catch

Stephanie and Samantha are friends. Stephanie is nine years old, and Samantha is six. They are sitting outside on a blanket.

The girls are sitting next to a big apartment building. They look up. A little boy is crawling out a window. It is on the fourth floor.

Stephanie and Samantha pick up the blanket and run to the building. They hold the blanket under the window. Stephanie holds one side of the blanket, and Samantha holds the other side. "Hold on tight," Stephanie tells Samantha.

The boy's head, shoulders, and arms are out the window. He puts his leg out the window. Then he falls. Stephanie and Samantha catch him in the blanket.

Paramedics come. The boy is fine. "Lucky boy," the paramedics say. "Smart girls."

3. PRONUNCIATION

What are the letters? What sounds can they make? Listen to your teacher. Say the words.

k / ck / c	f	p	b	l	h
look	fine	pick	big	later	hold
pick	fall	put	boy	leg	head
luck	four	up	building	little	him
catch	floor		blanket	lucky	
come	friend				
crawl					

4. SPELLING

Write the word. Put the letters in the correct order.

1. einn   _____nine_____
2. sxi   _____
3. gril   _____

4. ookl   _____
5. ybo   _____
6. oorlf   _____

5. VOCABULARY

What do you see in the pictures? Write the words on the lines.

blanket   ~~fourth floor~~   crawl   shoulder   hold   paramedic

1. _fourth floor_

2. _____

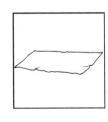

3. _____

4. _____

5. _____

6. _____

6. COMPREHENSION

Who is it? What is it? Write the letter of your answer on the line.

1. *They* are friends. __e__

2. *She* is nine years old. _____

3. The girls are sitting next to *it*. _____

4. *It* is on the fourth floor. _____

5. The girls hold *it* under the window. _____

6. The girls catch *him*. _____

7. *They* say, "Lucky boy. Smart girls." _____

   a. a big apartment building

   b. the paramedics

   c. Stephanie

   d. the little boy

   e. ~~Stephanie and Samantha~~

   f. the blanket

   g. the window

7. SPEAKING

Say the sentences and act them out.[1]

1. Look up.
2. Pick up the blanket.
3. Run to the apartment building.
4. Hold the blanket.
5. Hold on tight.
6. Catch the boy in the blanket.

8. WRITING

Your teacher will say the sentences in Exercise 7 (in any order). Listen to each sentence. Then copy it on your own paper.

---

[1] The directions for this activity are on page 87.

UNIT 6

Fufu Returns

1. PRE-READING

- Look at the picture. What do you see?
- Say the words.
- Watch your teacher write the words.
- Copy the words onto the picture.

2. READING

- Listen to your teacher read the story. Look at the pictures.
- Listen to your teacher read the story again. Look at the words.

1

Fufu is a beautiful cat.

2

She lives with Mrs. Romano.

3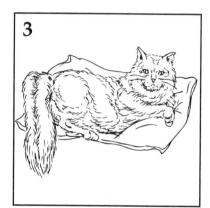

Fufu is happy at Mrs. Romano's house.

4

In the morning, she sits at her favorite window.

5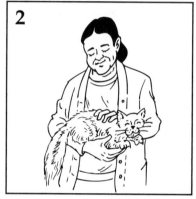

In the afternoon, she sleeps on her favorite chair.

6

In the evening, she eats from her favorite dish.

7

Then Mrs. Romano gets a dog. His name is Bruno.

8

In the morning, Bruno sits at Fufu's favorite window.

9

In the afternoon, he sleeps on Fufu's favorite chair.

10

In the evening, he eats from Fufu's favorite dish.

11

Fufu is not happy at Mrs. Romano's house. Fufu leaves.

12

Mrs. Romano looks everywhere for Fufu, but she can't find her. Fufu is gone.

13

Bruno lives with Mrs. Romano for eight years.

14

Then he dies.

15

The next day, Mrs. Romano opens the door, and there is Fufu. A male cat and three kittens are with her.

16

Fufu and her family walk into Mrs. Romano's house.

17

Fufu jumps up on her favorite chair.

18

Fufu is home.

- **Read the story again.**

Fufu Returns

Fufu is a beautiful cat. She lives with Mrs. Romano. Fufu is happy at Mrs. Romano's house. In the morning, she sits at her favorite window. In the afternoon, she sleeps on her favorite chair. In the evening, she eats from her favorite dish.

Then Mrs. Romano gets a dog. His name is Bruno. In the morning, Bruno sits at Fufu's favorite window. In the afternoon, he sleeps on Fufu's favorite chair. In the evening, he eats from Fufu's favorite dish. Fufu is not happy at Mrs. Romano's house. Fufu leaves.

Mrs. Romano looks everywhere for Fufu, but she can't find her. Fufu is gone.

Bruno lives with Mrs. Romano for eight years. Then he dies.

The next day, Mrs. Romano opens the door, and there is Fufu. A male cat and three kittens are with her. Fufu and her family walk into Mrs. Romano's house. Fufu jumps up on her favorite chair.

Fufu is home.

3. PRONUNCIATION

What are the letters? What sounds can they make? Listen to your teacher.
Say the words.

i
is
his
live
with
sit

a
at
cat
can't
has
happy

e / ee / ea
he
she
sleep
three
eat

u / o
up
jump
but
from

4. SPELLING

Listen to your teacher say the words. Write the missing letters. Then copy
the words.

1. ha _p_ p _y_   _happy_

2. ho __ s __   _____

3. fi __ d   _____

4. ei __ h __   _____

5. ye __ r   _____

6. da __   _____

5. VOCABULARY

What do you see in the pictures? Write the words on the lines.

dish   ~~male~~   leave   kitten   jump

1. _male_

2. _____

3. _____

4. _____

5. _____

6. COMPREHENSION

Which sentence is correct? Circle a or b.

1. **a.** Fufu is a beautiful dog.
   (b.) Fufu is a beautiful cat.
2. **a.** Fufu lives with Mr. Romano.
   b. Fufu lives with Mrs. Romano.
3. **a.** Fufu has a favorite window, a favorite bed, and a favorite dish.
   b. Fufu has a favorite window, a favorite chair, and a favorite dish.
4. **a.** Mrs. Romano gets a dog.
   b. Mrs. Romano gets a bird.
5. **a.** The dog sleeps in Fufu's favorite dish.
   b. The dog eats from Fufu's favorite dish.
6. **a.** The dog lives with Mrs. Romano for eight years.
   b. The dog lives with Mrs. Romano for two years.

7. WRITING / SPEAKING

Fufu has a favorite chair, window, and dish. What are your favorites?

A. Complete the sentences. Then read your sentences to a partner. For example:

My favorite color is _____blue_____.

Now write your answers.

1. My favorite color is _____.
2. My favorite fruit is _____.
3. My favorite place is _____.
4. My favorite activity is _____.
5. My favorite person is _____.

B. Tell your teacher your favorites. Your teacher will write your favorites on the board. For example:

	Color	*Fruit*	*Place*	*Activity*	*Person*
Abel:	red	strawberry	store	playing soccer	my girlfriend
Misuk:	yellow	peach	my house	cooking	my son

Not Too Small

1. PRE-READING

- Look at the picture. What do you see?
- Say the words.
- Watch your teacher write the words.
- Copy the words onto the picture.

2. READING

- Listen to your teacher read the story. Look at the pictures.
- Listen to your teacher read the story again. Look at the words.

Justin is 14 years old. He is a high school student.

He wants to play football at his school.

He goes to football practice. The boys are lifting weights.

Justin tries to lift the weights. He can't. He is too small.

The boys laugh. "You can't play football! You're too small!" they say.

Justin leaves football practice.

He is walking home. He is walking next to a lake.

A car goes off the road.

It goes into the lake.

10

It goes under the water.

11

A man is in the car.

12

Justin jumps into the water. He swims to the car.

13

He opens the car door. He pulls the man out of the car.

14

Then he pulls him out of the water. The man is OK.

15

Justin can't lift weights. He is too small.

16

He can't play football. He is too small.

17

But he can swim,

18

and he can save a man's life. He is not too small.

• Read the story again.

Not Too Small

Justin is 14 years old. He is a high school student. He wants to play football at his school.

He goes to football practice. The boys are lifting weights. Justin tries to lift the weights. He can't. He is too small.

The boys laugh. "You can't play football! You're too small!" they say.

Justin leaves football practice. He is walking home. He is walking next to a lake.

A car goes off the road. It goes into the lake. It goes under the water. A man is in the car.

Justin jumps into the water. He swims to the car. He opens the car door. He pulls the man out of the car. Then he pulls him out of the water. The man is OK.

Justin can't lift weights. He is too small. He can't play football. He is too small. But he can swim, and he can save a man's life. He is not too small.

3. PRONUNCIATION

What are the letters? What sounds can they make? Listen to your teacher. Say the words.

a / ay / ey	a / au	a / o	o / oa	o / oo / ou / u
save	at	water	OK	to
lake	can't	small	old	too
say	man	walk	open	school
play	practice	off	goes	you
they	laugh		home	student
			road	

4. SPELLING

Listen to your teacher say the words. Write the missing letters. Then copy the words.

1. sc _h_ o _o_ l   _school_

2. pla ___   _____

3. pra ___ t ___ ce   _____

4. bo ___ s   _____

5. sm ___ l ___   _____

6. wa ___ k   _____

5. VOCABULARY

What do you see in the pictures? Write the words on the lines.

football   t̶a̶k̶e̶   weights   road   laugh   pull

1. _lake_   2. _____   3. _____

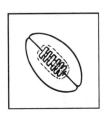

4. _____   5. _____   6. _____

6. COMPREHENSION

Who is it? What is it? Write your answer on the line.

Justin   the boys   the man   the car

1. *He* is 14 years old.   Justin

2. *It* goes under the water. _____

3. *They* tell Justin, "You can't play football." _____

4. *He* is in the car. _____

5. *He* is a high school student. _____

6. Justin pulls *him* out of the car. _____

7. *It* goes off the road. _____

8. *They* laugh at Justin. _____

7. SPEAKING

Listen to your teacher. Say the sentences. Then sing the sentences with your teacher. (The tune is "Happy Birthday.")

1. He wants to lift weights
   He wants to lift weights
   He wants to lift weights
   But he can't—he's too small.

2. He walks out the door
   He walks out the door
   He walks out the door
   And he starts walking home.

3. A car goes off the road
   A car goes off the road
   A car goes off the road
   And goes into the lake.

4. He jumps in the lake
   He jumps in the lake
   He jumps in the lake
   And he saves the man's life.

8. WRITING

Your teacher will read four sentences from the song (in any order). Listen to each sentence. Then copy it on your own paper.

UNIT 8

Mario's Rabbits

---

1. PRE-READING

- Look at the picture. What do you see?
- Say the words.
- Watch your teacher write the words.
- Copy the words onto the picture.

2. READING

- Listen to your teacher read the story. Look at the pictures.
- Listen to your teacher read the story again. Look at the words.

1

Mario wants a pet. He doesn't want a dog. He doesn't want a cat. He doesn't want a bird.

2

He wants a rabbit.

3

He buys two rabbits.

4

Are the rabbits male or female? Mario doesn't know.

5

In one month, Mario has eight rabbits.

6

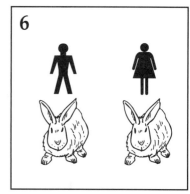

Now Mario knows: One rabbit is male, and the other rabbit is female.

7

In three months, Mario has 14 rabbits. It's OK; Mario likes rabbits.

8

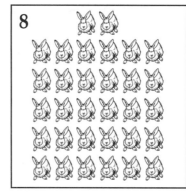

In six months, Mario has 32 rabbits. It's OK; Mario likes rabbits.

9

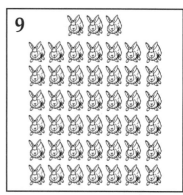

In nine months, Mario has 45 rabbits. It's OK; Mario likes rabbits.

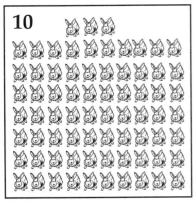

10

In one year, Mario has 73 rabbits. Now it's not OK.

11

There are rabbits everywhere in Mario's house.

12

They are in the kitchen and in the bathroom.

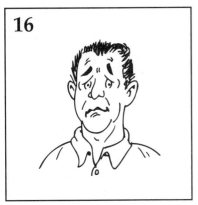

13

They are in the living room and in the bedrooms.

14

They are on Mario's bed, and in Mario's bed, and under Mario's bed.

15

They eat his sofa.

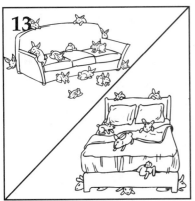

16

"I like rabbits," Mario says. "But I don't want 73 rabbits!"

17

People come to Mario's house. They take the rabbits.

18

Mario keeps one rabbit. He keeps only one.

• Read the story again.

Mario's Rabbits

Mario wants a pet. He doesn't want a dog. He doesn't want a cat. He doesn't want a bird. He wants a rabbit. He buys two rabbits. Are the rabbits male or female? Mario doesn't know.

In one month, Mario has eight rabbits. Now Mario knows: One rabbit is male, and the other rabbit is female. In three months, Mario has 14 rabbits. It's OK; Mario likes rabbits. In six months, Mario has 32 rabbits. It's OK; Mario likes rabbits. In nine months, Mario has 45 rabbits. It's OK; Mario likes

rabbits. In one year, Mario has 73 rabbits. Now it's not OK.

There are rabbits everywhere in Mario's house. They are in the kitchen and in the bathroom. They are in the living room and in the bedrooms. They are on Mario's bed, and in Mario's bed, and under Mario's bed. They eat his sofa. "I like rabbits," Mario says. "But I don't want 73 rabbits!"

People come to Mario's house. They take the rabbits. Mario keeps one rabbit. He keeps only one.

3. PRONUNCIATION

What are the letters? What sounds can they make? Listen to your teacher. Say the words.

s
sofa
house
likes
keeps
months

s
is
his
has
rooms
doesn't

b
bird
buy
bed
but

d
doesn't
dog
don't

m
Mario
male
month
room

n
now
under
only
in
one

4. SPELLING

Listen to your teacher say the words. Write the missing letters. Then copy the words.

1. w _a_ nt   _want_

2. do __ sn' __   _____

3. __ now   _____

4. b __ y   _____

5. o __ h __ r   _____

6. pe __ p __ e   _____

7. ho __ s __   _____

8. onl __   _____

5. VOCABULARY

Complete the sentences with the words below. Write your answer on the line.

pet   ~~male~~   female   month   sofa   keeps

1. A boy is _____ male _____.

2. A girl is _____.

3. In the living room, you sit on a chair or on the _____.

4. Mario has 73 rabbits. He gives 72 rabbits to other people. He _____ one rabbit.

5. There are usually 30 or 31 days in a _____.

6. A dog, cat, or bird in your house is a _____.

6. COMPREHENSION

Which word is correct? Circle your answer.

1. Mario wants a (bird / (rabbit)).

2. He buys (two / 73) rabbits.

3. He (likes / doesn't like) rabbits.

4. In one year, Mario has (45 / 73) rabbits.

5. The rabbits are everywhere in Mario's (garage / house).

6. People (buy / take) the rabbits.

7. Mario keeps (one rabbit / two rabbits).

7. WRITING / SPEAKING

Rabbits are in Mario's living room, kitchen, bathroom, and bedrooms. What things are usually in those rooms? (Not rabbits!)

Make four lists. Write as many words as you can. Then tell your teacher your words. Your teacher will write the words on the board.

Things in the living room	Things in the kitchen	Things in the bathroom	Things in the bedroom
sofa	_____	_____	_____
_____	_____	_____	_____
_____	_____	_____	_____
_____	_____	_____	_____
_____	_____	_____	_____

No Brakes!

---

1. PRE-READING

- Look at the picture. What do you see?
- Say the words.
- Watch your teacher write the words.
- Copy the words onto the picture.

2. READING

- Listen to your teacher read the story. Look at the pictures.
- Listen to your teacher read the story again. Look at the words.

Ann is driving her car on the highway.

A truck is in front of her.

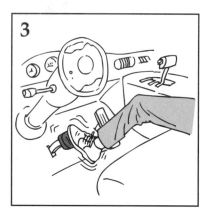

Ann wants to slow down. She steps on the brake.

Her car doesn't slow down. It goes faster.

Ann passes the truck.

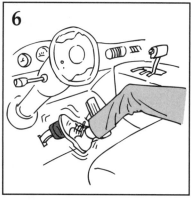

She steps on the brake again.

Her car doesn't slow down. It goes faster.

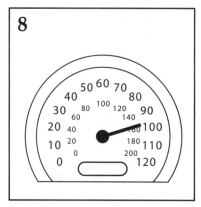

Ann's car goes 60, then 70, then 80, then 90, and then 100 miles per hour.

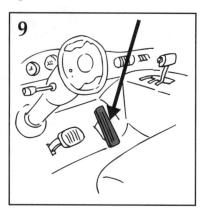

The accelerator is stuck.

10

Ann has a cell phone. She calls 911. "Help!" she says. "I can't stop my car!"

11

A police officer comes.

12

He drives in front of Ann's car. Now both cars are going 100 miles per hour.

13

The police officer slows down to 90 miles per hour. Ann's car hits the police car. Now both cars are going 90 miles per hour.

14

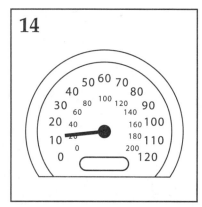

The police officer slows down to 80, to 70, to 60, to 50, to 40, to 30, to 20, and to 10 miles per hour. Ann's car slows down, too.

15

Finally, the police car stops. Ann's car stops, too.

16

Ann gets out of her car.

17

She hugs the police officer and says, "Thank you."

18

Then she kicks her car.

• Read the story again.

No Brakes!

Ann is driving her car on the highway. A truck is in front of her. Ann wants to slow down. She steps on the brake. Her car doesn't slow down. It goes faster.

Ann passes the truck. She steps on the brake again. Her car doesn't slow down. It goes faster. Ann's car goes 60, then 70, then 80, then 90, and then 100 miles per hour. The accelerator is stuck.

Ann has a cell phone. She calls 911. "Help!" she says. "I can't stop my car!"

A police officer comes. He drives in front of Ann's car. Now both cars are going 100 miles per hour.

The police officer slows down to 90 miles per hour. Ann's car hits the police car. Now both cars are going 90 miles per hour. The police officer slows down to 80, to 70, to 60, to 50, to 40, to 30, to 20, and to 10 miles per hour. Ann's car slows down, too.

Finally, the police car stops. Ann's car stops, too.

Ann gets out of her car. She hugs the police officer and says, "Thank you." Then she kicks her car.

3. PRONUNCIATION

Listen to your teacher. Say the numbers.

ten (10)	forty (40)	seventy (70)	one hundred (100)
twenty (20)	fifty (50)	eighty (80)	
thirty (30)	sixty (60)	ninety (90)	

4. SPELLING

Write the numbers.

80	_____	90	_____
50	_____	70	_____
30	_____	10	_____
40	_____	100	_____
20	_____	60	_____

5. VOCABULARY

What do you see in the pictures? Write the words on the lines.

~~highway~~   accelerator   pass   hug   brake   kick

1. *highway*_____

2. _____

3. _____

4. _____

5. _____

6. _____

6. COMPREHENSION

Complete the sentences. Write the letter of your answer on the line.

1. Ann steps on the brake, __b__

2. She calls 911, _____

3. The police officer slows down to 90 miles per hour, _____

4. The police car stops, _____

5. Ann gets out of her car, _____

a. and Ann's car stops, too.

b. and her car goes faster.

c. and a police officer comes.

d. and then she kicks it.

e. and Ann's car hits the police car.

7. SPEAKING

Say the sentences and act them out.[1]

1. Drive the car.
2. Step on the brake.
3. Pass the truck.
4. Call 911.
5. Get out of the car.
6. Kick the car.

8. WRITING

Your teacher will say the sentences in Exercise 7 (in any order). Listen to each sentence. Then copy it on your own paper.

---

[1] The directions for this activity are on page 89.

An Expensive Vacation

---

1. PRE-READING

- Look at the picture. What do you see?
- Say the words.
- Watch your teacher write the words.
- Copy the words onto the picture.

2. READING

- Listen to your teacher read the story. Look at the pictures.
- Listen to your teacher read the story again. Look at the words.

1

Don and Jack are on vacation. They are skiing.

2

They ski down the mountain.

3

Where are they? They don't know. They are lost.

4

The sun goes down.

5

It is very cold.

6

Don and Jack need to make a fire.

7

They have a lighter,

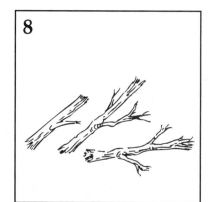

8

and they find some wood.

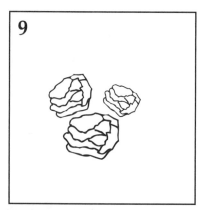

9

They need paper to start a fire.

10

They look in their pockets.

11

They don't have any paper, but they have some money. "Money is paper," they think.

12

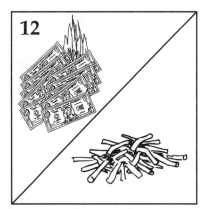

They burn their one-dollar bills. The fire doesn't start.

13

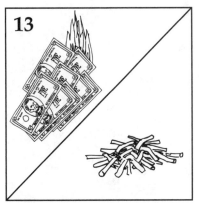

They burn their $5 bills. The fire doesn't start.

14

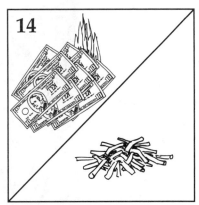

They burn their $10 bills. The fire doesn't start.

15

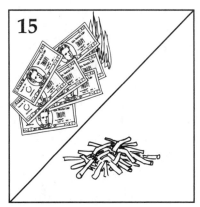

Finally, they burn their $20 bills.

16

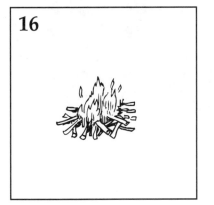

The fire starts! It burns all night.

17

People are looking for Don and Jack. They find them in the morning. Don and Jack are warm and fine.

18

"No more skiing vacations," they say. "Skiing is too expensive!"

• **Read the story again.**

An Expensive Vacation

Don and Jack are on vacation. They are skiing. They ski down the mountain. Where are they? They don't know. They are lost.

The sun goes down. It is very cold. Don and Jack need to make a fire. They have a lighter, and they find some wood. They need paper to start a fire.

They look in their pockets. They don't have any paper, but they have some money. "Money is paper," they think.

They burn their $1 bills. The fire doesn't start. They burn their $5 bills. The fire doesn't start. They burn their $10 bills. The fire doesn't start. Finally, they burn their $20 bills. The fire starts! It burns all night.

People are looking for Don and Jack. They find them in the morning. Don and Jack are warm and fine.

"No more skiing vacations," they say. "Skiing is too expensive!"

3. PRONUNCIATION

What are the letters? What sounds can they make? Listen to your teacher. Say the words.

o	o	ee / eo / i	a / ay / ey	ow / ou	or / ar
don't	on	see	make	now	for
no	Don	need	paper	down	morning
know	pocket	people	say	mountain	warm
goes	dollar	ski	they		
cold	not				

4. VOCABULARY

Complete the sentences with the words below. Write your answer on the line.

wood   fire   expensive

~~mountain~~ lost   bills

1. Don and Jack ski down the _____*mountain*_____ .

2. Where are they? They don't know. They are _____ .

3. It is very cold. They need to make a _____ .

4. To start the fire, they need a lighter, paper, and _____ .

5. They have money. They have $1, $5, $10, and $20 _____ .

6. They burn all their money. They say, "Skiing is _____!"

5. COMPREHENSION

One word in each sentence is not correct. Find the word and cross it out. Write the correct word.

1. Don and Jack are ~~swimming~~ . *skiing*

2. They need to make a lunch.

3. They look in their pockets, and they find some paper.

4. They spend their money.

5. The fire starts and burns all afternoon.

6. When people find Don and Jack, they are warm and sad.

6. WRITING / SPEAKING

Don and Jack are on vacation. They are skiing.

Imagine this: You are on vacation. Where are you? What are you doing? Draw a picture on your own paper. Under your picture, write where you are and what you are doing. Then share your picture with the class. For example:

I am in my village.
I am singing to the children.

The Parking Ticket

1. PRE-READING

- Look at the picture. What do you see?
- Say the words.
- Watch your teacher write the words.
- Copy the words onto the picture.

2. READING

- Listen to your teacher read the story. Look at the pictures.
- Listen to your teacher read the story again. Look at the words.

Colin is parking his car.

He is parking next to a sign. It says, "NO PARKING." He doesn't see the sign.

Later, Colin comes back to his car. A police officer is standing next to it. She is writing a ticket.

"No parking here," she says.

Colin doesn't want a ticket. Parking tickets are expensive.

He talks to the police officer. She smiles a little.

"I'm sorry," she says. "But I'm giving you a ticket."

Colin likes the police officer. He wants to see her again.

Every day Colin parks next to the "NO PARKING" sign.

10

Every day the police officer gives him a ticket.

11

Then Colin talks to her.

12

Colin gets a lot of parking tickets.

13

He pays a lot of money.

14

Love is expensive!

15

Finally, Colin asks the police officer, "Can you have dinner with me tonight?"

16

She says, "Yes," so they have dinner together.

17

One year later, Colin marries the police officer.

18

Now Colin has a wife—and no more parking tickets!

- **Read the story again.**

The Parking Ticket

Colin is parking his car. He is parking next to a sign. It says, "NO PARKING." He doesn't see the sign.

Later, Colin comes back to his car. A police officer is standing next to it. She is writing a ticket. "No parking here," she says.

Colin doesn't want a ticket. Parking tickets are expensive. He talks to the police officer. She smiles a little. "I'm sorry," she says. "But I'm giving you a ticket."

Colin likes the police officer. He wants to see her again.

Every day Colin parks next to the "NO PARKING" sign. Every day the police officer gives him a ticket. Then Colin talks to her. Colin gets a lot of parking tickets. He pays a lot of money. Love is expensive!

Finally, Colin asks the police officer, "Can you have dinner with me tonight?" She says, "Yes," so they have dinner together.

One year later, Colin marries the police officer.

Now Colin has a wife—and no more parking tickets!

3. PRONUNCIATION

What are the letters? What sounds can they make? Listen to your teacher. Say the words.

i	i	a / ay / ey	a	o / u	e / ay
like	ticket	later	ask	love	next
wife	give	day	back	money	get
write	him	pay	stand	come	yes
smile	with	say	have	doesn't	says
sign	dinner	they	has	much	

4. VOCABULARY

What do you see in the pictures? Write the words on the lines.

sign   a parking ticket   a lot of parking tickets
~~smile~~   expensive   marry

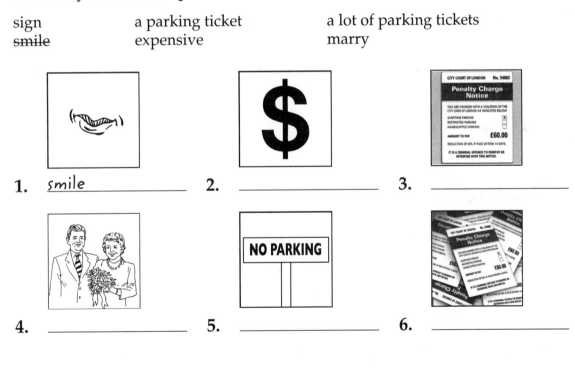

1. _smile_   2. _____   3. _____

4. _____   5. _____   6. _____

5. COMPREHENSION

Answer the questions. Complete the sentences.

1. Where does Colin park?

   He parks ___ *next to* ___ a "NO PARKING" sign.

2. Who is standing next to Colin's car?

A _____ is standing next to it.

3. What does she give Colin?

She gives him a _____.

4. How many tickets does Colin get?

He gets a _____ of tickets.

5. Why does Colin park next to the "NO PARKING" sign?

He wants to _____ the police officer.

6. When does Colin marry the police officer?

He marries her one year _____.

6. SPEAKING

Listen to your teacher. Say the sentences. Then sing the sentences with your teacher. (The tune is "Row, Row, Row Your Boat.")

Park, park, park your car,
But don't park by the sign.
You will get a ticket there,
And you will pay a fine.[1]

7. WRITING

A. Copy four sentences from the story on your own paper.

B. Change each sentence so one word is not correct. For example:

motorcycle
Colin is parking his ~~car~~.

C. Read your sentences to a partner. Your partner will tell you which word is not correct.

---

[1] You will pay a fine. = You will pay money.

The Present

1. PRE-READING

- Look at the picture. What do you see?
- Say the words.
- Watch your teacher write the words.
- Copy the words onto the picture.

2. READING

- Listen to your teacher read the story. Look at the pictures.
- Listen to your teacher read the story again. Look at the words.

1

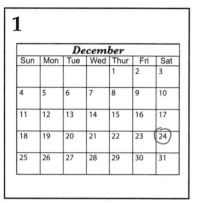

December						
Sun	Mon	Tue	Wed	Thur	Fri	Sat
				1	2	3
4	5	6	7	8	9	10
11	12	13	14	15	16	17
18	19	20	21	22	23	24
25	26	27	28	29	30	31

It is December 24, the day before a big holiday.

2

Many people are shopping. They are buying presents for their families and friends.

3

In one store, there is a long line of people. They are waiting to pay.

4

Mrs. Park is waiting in line. She is holding a toy.

5

It is a present for her son.

6

It is expensive. It is $85.

7

Mrs. Park gives the toy to the cashier.

8

Then she looks in her purse. There is no money in her purse.

9

She looks in her pockets. There is no money in her pockets. Her money is gone.

10

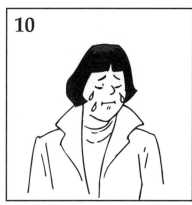

She begins to cry.

11

A man is standing at the end of the line. He opens his wallet. He takes out $20. He passes the money to the young woman in front of him.

12

The young woman opens her purse. She takes out $10. She passes the $30 to the boy in front of her.

13

The boy looks in his pocket. He finds $5. He passes the $35 to the woman in front of him.

14

The woman opens her purse. She takes out $40. She passes the $75 to the young man in front of her.

15

The young man opens his wallet. He takes out $10. He gives the $85 to the cashier.

16

The cashier gives the toy to Mrs. Park.

17

Mrs. Park smiles at the people in line. "Thank you," she says. "Thank you very much."

18

She goes home with the present for her son.

• **Read the story again.**

The Present

It is December 24, the day before a big holiday. Many people are shopping. They are buying presents for their families and friends.

In one store, there is a long line of people. They are waiting to pay.

Mrs. Park is waiting in line. She is holding a toy. It is a present for her son. It is expensive. It is $85.

Mrs. Park gives the toy to the cashier. Then she looks in her purse. There is no money in her purse. She looks in her pockets. There is no money in her pockets. Her money is gone. She begins to cry.

A man is standing at the end of the line. He opens his wallet. He takes out $20. He passes the money to the young woman in front of him.

The young woman opens her purse. She takes out $10. She passes the $30 to the boy in front of her.

The boy looks in his pocket. He finds $5. He passes the $35 to the woman in front of him.

The woman opens her purse. She takes out $40. She passes the $75 to the young man in front of her.

The young man opens his wallet. He takes out $10. He gives the $85 to the cashier. The cashier gives the toy to Mrs. Park.

Mrs. Park smiles at the people in line. "Thank you," she says. "Thank you very much."

She goes home with the present for her son.

3. PRONUNCIATION

What are the letters? What sounds can they make? Listen to your teacher. Say the words.

p	b	f	f / v	t	sh
pay	buy	for	of	to	shop
people	boy	before	very	take	she
pocket		family	give	twenty	cashier
present		friend		ten	
purse		fifty			
expensive		five			

4. VOCABULARY

Complete the sentences with the words below. Write your answer on the line.

holiday   line   present   ~~toys~~   wallet   pass

1. Children like to play with _____ toys _____.

2. You are shopping at a store. You are waiting to pay. You stand in

   _____.

3. In many countries, people don't work on January 1. It is a

   _____.

4. A man puts his money in his pocket or in his _____.

5. It is your friend's birthday. You buy something for your friend. It is a

   _____.

6. You are eating with your family. A dish with rice is on the table. You want

   more rice. You say, "Please _____ the rice."

5. COMPREHENSION

Which sentence is correct? Circle a or b.

1. (a.) It is December 24, the day before a big holiday.
   b. It is December 26, the day after a big holiday.

2. a. People are buying presents.
   b. People are buying food.

3. **a.** Mrs. Park is holding a book.
   b. Mrs. Park is holding a toy.

4. **a.** It is a present for her daughter.
   b. It is a present for her son.

5. **a.** Her money is gone.
   b. Her money is in her purse.

6. **a.** The people in line pay for the toy.
   b. The cashier pays for the toy.

6. WRITING

Copy the correct answers in Exercise 5 on your own paper. For example:

It is December 24, the day before a big holiday. People are . . .

7. SPEAKING

A. Listen to your teacher. Say the sentences.

1. Open your wallet. Take out some money. Pass the money to the young woman in front of you.
2. Open your purse. Take out some money. Pass the money to the boy in front of you.
3. Look in your pocket. Take out some money. Pass the money to the woman in front of you.
4. Open your purse. Take out some money. Pass the money to the young man in front of you.
5. Open your wallet. Take out some money. Give the money to the cashier.
6. Give the toy to Mrs. Park.
7. Smile at the people in line. Say, "Thank you."

B. Seven students (four male students and three female students) come to the front of the class. They stand in a line like this:

Mrs. Park   Cashier

C. Listen to your teacher. Say the sentences again. As you say the sentences, the people at the front of the class act out the story.

The Taxi Ride

---

1. PRE-READING

- Look at the picture. What do you see?
- Say the words.
- Watch your teacher write the words.
- Copy the words onto the picture.

2. READING

- Listen to your teacher read the story. Look at the pictures.
- Listen to your teacher read the story again. Look at the words.

1

Clifton is three years old. He is with his mother and two brothers.

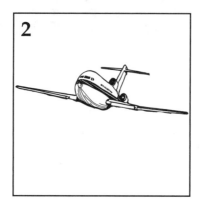

2

They are at an airport in New York. They are going on a trip.

3

Clifton sees a big yellow taxi. The taxi driver is standing next to the taxi.

4

Clifton likes to ride in taxis. He runs to the taxi.

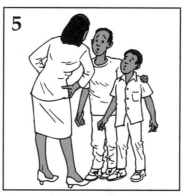

5

Clifton's mother is talking to Clifton's brothers. She doesn't see Clifton.

6

Clifton gets in the taxi. He sits in the front seat.

7

Then a woman gets in the taxi. She sits in the back seat.

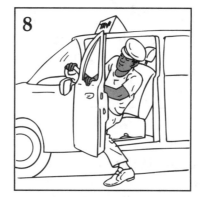

8

Then the taxi driver gets in the taxi.

9

The taxi driver thinks, "The little boy is with the woman. He is her son."

10

The woman thinks, "The little boy is with the taxi driver. He is his son."

11

The taxi driver drives for 30 minutes.

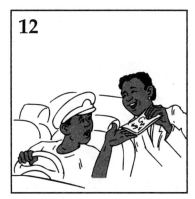

12

Then he stops. The woman pays the taxi driver and gets out of the taxi.

13

"Wait!" the taxi driver says. "Don't forget your son."

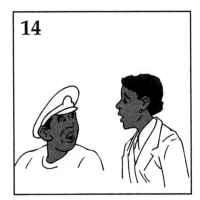

14

"My son?" the woman says. "He's not my son." "Oh, no!" the taxi driver says.

15

The taxi driver drives back to the airport with Clifton.

16

The taxi driver sees Clifton's mother. She is crying and talking to the police.

17

"Is he your son?" the taxi driver asks.
"Yes! He's my son," she says.

18

Clifton's mother is happy. The taxi driver is happy. Clifton is happy, too. He likes to ride in taxis.

• **Read the story again.**

The Taxi Ride

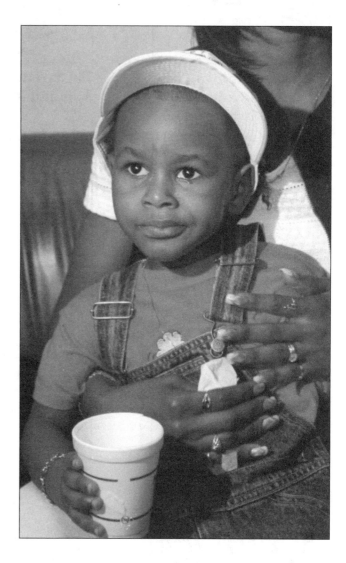

Clifton is three years old. He is with his mother and two brothers. They are at an airport in New York. They are going on a trip.

Clifton sees a big yellow taxi. The taxi driver is standing next to the taxi. Clifton likes to ride in taxis. He runs to the taxi. Clifton's mother is talking to Clifton's brothers. She doesn't see Clifton.

Clifton gets in the taxi. He sits in the front seat. Then a woman gets in the taxi. She sits in the back seat. Then the taxi driver gets in the taxi.

The taxi driver thinks, "The little boy is with the woman. He is her son." The woman thinks, "The little boy is with the taxi driver. He is his son."

The taxi driver drives for 30 minutes. Then he stops. The woman pays the taxi driver and gets out of the taxi.

"Wait!" the taxi driver says. "Don't forget your son."

"My son?" the woman says. "He's not my son."

"Oh, no!" the taxi driver says.

The taxi driver drives back to the airport with Clifton. The taxi driver sees Clifton's mother. She is crying and talking to the police.

"Is he your son?" the taxi driver asks.

"Yes! He's my son," she says.

Clifton's mother is happy. The taxi driver is happy. Clifton is happy, too. He likes to ride in taxis.

3. PRONUNCIATION

What are the letters? What sounds can they make? Listen to your teacher. Say the words.

s	s	th	th	p / pp	k / ck
see	years	three	the	pay	think
seat	brothers	think	they	police	drink
sit	taxis	thirty	then	happy	like
son	runs	with	mother	airport	talk
stand	drives		brother	trip	ask
stop	pays			stop	back

4. VOCABULARY

Which words go together? Write the letter of your answer on the line.

1. not my sister __c__

2. not small _____

3. not drive _____

4. not get in _____

5. not back _____

6. not smile _____

a. ride

b. front

c. my brother

d. cry

e. big

f. get out

5. COMPREHENSION

Complete the sentences. Circle a or b.

1. Clifton is
   a. 10 years old.
   b. three years old.

2. He is with his
   a. father and two sisters.
   b. mother and two brothers.

3. They are at
   a. a restaurant.
   b. an airport.

4. Clifton gets in a big
- **a.** yellow taxi.
- **b.** black car.

5. The taxi driver drives for
- **a.** 30 minutes.
- **b.** 10 minutes.

6. The taxi driver says to the woman, "Don't forget your
- **a.** change."
- **b.** son."

7. The taxi driver drives back to the airport with
- **a.** Clifton.
- **b.** the woman.

6. WRITING

Clifton likes to ride in taxis. What do you like to do?

Write three sentences on the lines. For example:

I like to watch movies.

1. _____

2. _____

3. _____

7. SPEAKING

A. **Read one of your sentences to the class. Listen as your classmates say their sentences. Try to remember their sentences.**

B. **Your teacher will point to a classmate. When the teacher points to that classmate, say what he or she likes to do. For example:**

"He likes to play the piano."

"She likes to swim."

Internet Friend

---

1. PRE-READING

- Look at the picture. What do you see?
- Say the words.
- Watch your teacher write the words.
- Copy the words onto the picture.

2. READING

- Listen to your teacher read the story. Look at the pictures.
- Listen to your teacher read the story again. Look at the words.

It is 3 A.M. in a town in Scotland.

Ken Walker is not sleeping. He has a bad headache.

He goes to his computer. He wants to "talk" to people on the Internet. He doesn't want to think about his headache.

Ken999:
Hello! My name is Ken Walker.

A A A A ☺▾   send

"Hello!" he types. "My name is Ken Walker."

It is 10 P.M. in the United States. A man in the United States answers. "Hello," he types. "My name is Dick Eastman."

Suddenly Ken feels very, very sick.

Ken999:
HAVE PROBLEM. NEED HELP.

A A A A ☺▾   send

He types, "HAVE PROBLEM. NEED HELP."

Dick011:
Are you serious?

A A A A ☺▾   send

Dick types, "Are you serious?"

Ken999:
Yes. Please help me.

A A A A ☺▾   send

"Yes," Ken types. "Please help me."

80   Unit 14

10

Dick011:
Where are you?

A A A A ☺▾ send

"Where are you?" Dick asks.

11

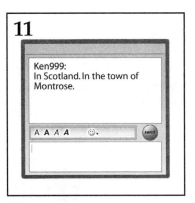

Ken999:
In Scotland. In the town of Montrose.

A A A A ☺▾ send

"In Scotland. In the town of Montrose," Ken types.

12

Dick calls an operator in Scotland. "A man in Montrose needs help," he says. "His name is Ken Walker."

13

Ken999:
I feel very tired. Please help me. I am alone.

A A A A ☺▾ send

"I feel very tired," Ken types. "Please help me. I am alone."

14

Dick011:
No, Ken, you are not alone. I am with you. Ken, are you there? Ken?

A A A A ☺▾ send

"No, Ken, you are not alone," Dick types. "I am with you. Ken, are you there? Ken?"

15

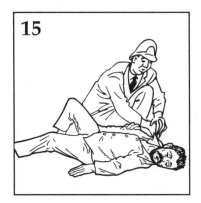

The operator calls the police in Montrose. It is a very small town. The police know Ken Walker. They walk to his house and open the door. Ken is lying on the floor.

16

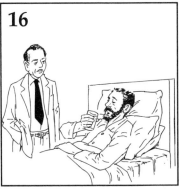

The police take Ken to the hospital. Doctors give him medicine. He is OK.

17

Ken goes home and gets on the Internet. He writes Dick Eastman.

18

Ken999:
Hello, Dick. I am fine now. Thank you, my dear Internet friend.

A A A A ☺▾ send

"Hello, Dick," he types. "I am fine now. Thank you, my dear Internet friend."

- Read the story again.

Internet Friend

It is 3 A.M. in a town in Scotland. Ken Walker is not sleeping. He has a bad headache.

He goes to his computer. He wants to "talk" to people on the Internet. He doesn't want to think about his headache.

"Hello!" he types. "My name is Ken Walker."

It is 10 P.M. in the United States. A man in the United States answers. "Hello," he types. "My name is Dick Eastman."

Suddenly Ken feels very, very sick. He types, "HAVE PROBLEM. NEED HELP."

Dick types, "Are you serious?"

"Yes," Ken types. "Please help me."

"Where are you?" Dick asks.

"In Scotland. In the town of Montrose," Ken types.

Dick calls an operator in Scotland. "A man in Montrose needs help," he says. "His name is Ken Walker."

"I feel very tired," Ken types. "Please help me. I am alone."

"No, Ken, you are not alone," Dick types. "I am with you. Ken, are you there? Ken?"

The operator calls the police in Montrose. It is a very small town. The police know Ken Walker. They walk to his house and open the door. Ken is lying on the floor.

The police take Ken to the hospital. Doctors give him medicine. He is OK.

Ken goes home and gets on the Internet. He writes Dick Eastman. "Hello, Dick," he types. "I am fine now. Thank you, my dear Internet friend."

3. PRONUNCIATION

What are the letters? What sounds can they make? Listen to your teacher. Say the words.

o / ow	ow / ou	i / y	o / a	ee / eo	e / ie / ay
go	now	fine	on	sleep	ten
goes	town	write	not	feel	Ken
open	house	my	hospital	need	get
home		type	problem	people	friend
no		lying	want		says
know					

4. VOCABULARY

Which words go together? Write the letter of your answer on the line.

1. not a city ___d___   **a.** a headache

2. not A.M. _____   **b.** serious

3. not a backache _____   **c.** lying

4. not write _____   ~~**d.** a town~~

5. not funny _____   **e.** type

6. not sitting or standing _____   **f.** P.M.

5. COMPREHENSION

Complete the sentences. Circle a or b.

1. It is 3 A.M. in
   (a.) Scotland.
   b. Australia.
2. Ken Walker has a bad
   a. cold.
   b. headache.
3. He wants to "talk" to people on the
   a. telephone.
   b. Internet.

4. Suddenly Ken feels very, very
   a. sick.
   b. sad.

5. He types, "Have problem. Need
   a. medicine."
   b. help."

6. The man in the United States calls
   a. Ken's family.
   b. an operator in Scotland.

7. The police take Ken to the
   a. hospital.
   b. police station.

8. Doctors give him medicine, and he is
   a. OK.
   b. serious.

6. SPEAKING

Sit with a partner and read the conversation aloud. Student A begins.

Student A	Student B
1. Hello!	Hello!
2. My name is Ken.	My name is Dick.
3. I have a problem. I need help.	Are you serious?
4. Yes. I'm sick.	Where are you?
5. I'm in Scotland.	I'm calling for help.
6. I'm alone.	No, you're not alone. I'm with you.
7. I'm fine now. Thank you, my dear Internet friend.	You're welcome.

7. WRITING

Copy the correct answers in Exercise 5 on your own paper. For example:

It is 3 A.M. in Scotland. Ken Walker has a bad . . .

To the Teacher

The original newspaper and magazine versions of *All New Very Easy True Stories* contain information that could not be included in the adaptations. Sometimes the information was too complicated to include; sometimes including it would have made the stories too long for the allotted space. On the other hand, the information—in many cases, the story behind the story—was just too interesting to leave out entirely, so it was decided that additional facts would be given here, in a special To the Teacher section.

As you will see from the sophistication of the language, this section is not meant to be read by students. If, however, you think the information adds interest or clarity to a story, you could share it with students. Also included here are specific teaching tips for some of the exercises.

Unit 1

GENESIO'S GIFT

Genesio Morlacci, an immigrant from Italy, opened a dry cleaning shop in the United States in the 1940s and operated it until the 1960s. After he sold his dry cleaning business, he worked part-time as a custodian at the University of Great Falls, Montana, the recipient of his estate.

Mr. Morlacci was known for his frugality. He and his wife, who had no children, lived in a small house next to the dry cleaning shop and rented out the basement for extra income. When his shirts became worn, he removed the collars and sewed them back on, frayed side down. The one luxury the Morlaccis allowed themselves during their lifetime was several trips to Italy.

Genesio's gift will generate $100,000 a year in scholarships. Described in his short obituary as having a "passion for education," Mr. Morlacci hoped his money would help others obtain the formal education he never had. He attended school in his native Italy for only three years.

Teaching Tip:
The pronunciation exercise contrasts the two sounds made by the letter *s* (the voiced [z] and the unvoiced [s]). You might want to have students place their fingertips on their throats to feel the vibration when they make the [z] sound and note the lack of vibration

when they make the [s] sound. Please keep in mind that the purpose of the pronunciation exercise is simply to make students aware that in English a letter can represent more than one sound, not to drill students into pronouncing the sounds perfectly.

Unit 2

THE SURPRISE

Ian had a key to Amy's flat in England, so when he arrived and she wasn't there, he let himself in and lay down on the sofa to sleep after his long flight. He assumed Amy was out for the evening. Then the phone rang. It was Amy, calling from Australia.

In an interview with the *London Mirror*, Amy described her arrival at Ian's apartment in Australia: "I knocked on Ian's door and one of his flatmates answered. He went white. He told me Ian had gone back to Britain to see me. I didn't believe him. But the truth hit me when I found Ian's rucksack and clothes missing. I sat on his bed and cried my eyes out. When I phoned Ian in Britain, he would not believe that I was calling from his flat." Both Ian and Amy had nonrefundable tickets, so Amy ended up spending two weeks in Australia while Ian spent two weeks in England.

Amy and Ian had both changed planes in Singapore. Later they realized that they had been at the Singapore airport at the same time, sitting in the same waiting area, without seeing each other.

Ian had flown to England with an engagement ring in his pocket. When Amy called from Australia, he proposed over the phone. She accepted.

Unit 3

HICCUP! HICCUP!

Charles Osborne was lifting the carcass of a butchered hog when he began to hiccup. The many doctors he consulted over the years are not sure why the lifting precipitated the hiccups. One doctor speculated that a blood vessel at the base of Osborne's brain burst during the exertion and damaged a nerve ending that controls breathing. In spite of hiccuping 20 times a minute, Osborne managed to live a fairly normal life. He had eight children and died at the age of 97, one year after he stopped hiccuping. He is in the *Guinness Book of*

World Records as the person who hiccuped for the longest time, although there is a man in North Carolina who could possibly break his record. That man has been hiccuping since a car accident in 1961.

Hiccuping is a reflex that results in uncontrollable spasms in the diaphragm and seems to serve no purpose. It is often triggered by irritations to the smooth muscle of the stomach or esophagus, which is why hiccuping is often preceded by eating. The irritated nerve sends a message to the reflex center in the brain, and nerves coming out of the center cause the spasms. Most home remedies work by stimulation of the same nerve course. Many doctors say the most effective remedy is swallowing a small amount of peanut butter or ice cream.

Teaching Tips:
Before beginning the unit, you might put the word *hiccup* on the board and demonstrate its meaning. If you then ask students to share remedies for stopping hiccups, they might come up with several that they will later read in the story. You might also ask students what the word for *hiccup* is in their native languages, as the word is onomatopoeic in many languages.

The speaking exercise is a Total Physical Response (TPR) activity.

These are suggested steps for a TPR activity:

1. Three students come to the front of the room. They stand with you, facing the class.
2. Say the sentences. After each sentence, you and the three students act it out. The three students return to their seats.
3. Repeat steps 1 and 2 with three different students. This can be done several times.
4. Three students come to the front of the room. Volunteers read the sentences aloud, or the class reads the sentences aloud. The students at the front of the room act the sentences out without your help.

Unit 4

WRONG NUMBER

Mary was walking back into the living room when she heard a loud noise and then saw the glass in her living room window shatter. The wall crumbled and fell on the chair she had just left. "The phone ringing at that particular time?" Mary told the *Columbus Dispatch*. "That's just one of those things people would never believe."

Mary's century-old house sits on the curve of a highway. This was not the first time a car missed the curve, crashed into the house, and narrowly missed injuring someone. In the early 1970s, a car left the road and hit both the front porch and a pickup truck that was parked in the driveway. The truck belonged to Mary's nephew, who was living at the house with Mary and his mother. He was on his way out to the truck when he remembered that he had not said good-bye to his mother. "As soon as he walked away from his truck and into the house," his mother remembers, "someone crashed and took out his truck and the porch. Perhaps we're all blessed."

Teaching Tips:
You may also wish to try the following speaking exercise, a TPR (Total Physical Response) activity. First, put four chairs at the front of the room and write these sentences on the board:

- You are tired.
- Sit down.
- Say "Ah."
- Get up.
- Walk to the kitchen.
- Answer the phone.
- Walk back to the living room.
- You are shocked.

Please see the suggested steps for using the sentences in a TPR activity under Teaching Tips in Unit 3.

An alternate writing exercise might be a pair dictation. Write the following sentences on the board:

1. Mary sits down.
2. The phone rings.
3. She goes into the kitchen.
4. She answers the phone.
5. It is a wrong number.
6. A car crashes into her house.
7. The wall falls on her chair.
8. Mary is shocked.

Students sit in pairs. Student A turns away from the board. Student B dictates sentences 1–4 to Student A, and Student A writes them. Then Student B turns away from the board, and Student A dictates sentences 5–8 to Student B. Finally, both students turn to the board to check their work.

Unit 5

THE CATCH

The boy who crawled out the window was four years old—only two years younger than Samantha, one of the girls who caught him. The boy landed with such force that the blanket was ripped out of the girls' hands, and he hit the ground, landing on his back. Because the blanket broke his fall, he had only a few bruises.

There is a third "smart girl" in the story. Randilyn, Samantha's nine-year-old sister, ran into the apartment building. After determining which apartment the boy lived in, she knocked, then pounded, then kicked on the apartment door. She was unable to wake the boy's mother, who was taking a nap.

The girls told the *Toronto Sun* they got the idea for using the blanket from an episode of the cartoon show *Pipi Longstocking*. In the episode, someone is saved from a burning building by jumping into a blanket. Pipi Longstocking, the character created by Swedish writer Astrid Lindgren in 1944, is an independent and adventurous nine-year-old girl with unruly orange pigtails, crazy socks, and superhuman strength.

The girls, who are Canadian, appeared as guests on several television shows in the United States and were honored by a Toronto baseball team for their great catch.

Teaching Tips:
For the speaking exercise: This is a TPR (Total Physical Response) activity. Please see the suggested steps under Teaching Tips in Unit 3.

For the writing exercise: Students who are confident writers may wish to cover the sentences with a piece of paper and write from memory, making the activity a dictation rather than a copying exercise.

Unit 6

FUFU RETURNS

Fufu's owner, who lives in Sicily, told the newspaper *Giornale di Sicilia* she was certain the cat who appeared on her doorstep was Fufu. Fufu had lost two teeth in a fall from a tree, and she had lost the tip of her tail in an accident with a door. The cat on her doorstep was missing two teeth and the tip of her tail. Furthermore, the owner reported, "When I let her in, she went straight to her favorite chair—it hadn't been moved all the while she was away."

Fufu's owner has no idea where Fufu was living during the eight years she was missing but believes she might have stayed close to home. In an article in the *London Express* (titled "Return of the Sourpuss") the owner stated, "I think it is no coincidence that she returned such a short time after the dog died."

Teaching Tip:
For the writing / speaking exercise, you write students' favorites on the board in a chart. (You will probably want to write only five or six students' answers on the board.) Once the words are on the board, you can expand the activity by asking questions based on the chart, for example: "What is Abel's favorite color?" ("It's red.")

Unit 7

NOT TOO SMALL

At 5 feet 3 inches and 130 pounds, Justin couldn't lift as much weight as the other football players at practice. When they teased him, he was so upset that he abruptly left practice. As he walked home, dejected and worried, he began to regret his decision. "The coach will be mad," he thought. "Why did I leave?"

Just at that moment, a gold Lincoln veered off the road in front of him, went through a chain-link fence, and shot into a retention pond (described in the story as a "lake"). The car began to sink immediately, grill first. "It happened so fast," Justin told the *St. Petersburg Times* in Florida. "I turned my head and bam!—the car was in the water." Justin was helped in the rescue by two other passersby, who also jumped into the cold, alligator-infested water. (The woman in the photo is Justin's mother.)

The 82-year-old driver of the car was in good condition and had only minor injuries.

Teaching Tip:

As an alternate writing / speaking exercise, you might ask students to share information about what they can do. Begin by writing this sentence on the board: "Justin can swim." Ask them to complete this sentence on their own paper: "I can _____." They might write three or four sentences. Ask them to read one of their sentences aloud. Then make a list of things students can do on the board. For example:

    Ana   cook

    Tony   fix cars

    Setsuko   take good photos

You can then ask questions based on the list, for example, "What can Ana do?" ("She can cook.") or "Can Ana fix cars?" ("No, she can't. But she can cook.")

Unit 8

MARIO'S RABBITS

The Louisiana man who bought the rabbits lived alone and wanted some company. He got more company than he bargained for when the rabbits did what rabbits are famous for: they multiplied like rabbits. With full run of the house, the rabbits burrowed into sofas, chairs, and mattresses, and they chewed on furniture and electrical wires. Mario finally called the SPCA (Society for the Prevention of Cruelty to Animals) when he became ill while cleaning up after the rabbits.

It took four SPCA workers almost a day to catch the rabbits. At the end of the day, the crew was still not sure they had caught them all. They left out water and rabbit food in case they had missed a few rabbits and intended to check back in a day or two.

"Mario" is a pseudonym. The rabbit owner was embarrassed that he had neglected to ask the gender of the rabbits when he bought them. He asked the *Times-Picayune* newspaper, which reported the story, to withhold his name, and the newspaper complied with his request. Animal experts, however, say that the man's chagrin was perhaps unwarranted. It is extremely difficult to determine the gender of a rabbit just by looking at it, so even if the man had asked about the rabbits' gender, he might have been given the wrong answer anyway. Experts also say that few people understand just how rapidly rabbits propagate. Females begin producing offspring at the age of five months, the gestation period is only one month, and litters are from 4 to 10 bunnies. So it is not surprising that a household of two unsupervised rabbits became a household of 73 in a year.

Teaching Tip:

An alternate speaking / writing activity would be to poll students about which pets they would like to have and record their answers in a chart on the board, for example:

	Dog	Cat	Bird	Rabbit	Two rabbits
Nelia	no	yes	yes	no	no
Uwe	yes	no	no	yes	no

You could then ask questions based on the chart, for example, "Does Nelia want a dog?" ("No, she doesn't.") As a follow-up writing activity, students could compose sentences based on the information in the chart, for example:

    Nelia doesn't want a dog.

    Uwe wants a rabbit.

Unit 9

NO BRAKES!

Ann (a pseudonym for the young woman in the story) was driving to Denver on Interstate 70 when she came up behind a truck and discovered she couldn't slow down. She tried to unstick the accelerator, but it was locked in place. She tried to shift into neutral, but the clutch wouldn't move, either. Next, she pulled on the emergency brake, but it didn't work. Finally, she tried to turn off the ignition. The key wouldn't budge. "My car had a mind of its own," she told the Associated Press. "It kept accelerating, and my foot wasn't even down on the gas."

For 45 minutes, she drove her 1997 Pontiac Sunfire at speeds up to 100 miles an hour, moving to the shoulder of the road three times to avoid hitting other vehicles. After she dialed 911, the highway was closed, so only her car and the police cars trailing her were on the road.

One of the police officers recalled an episode of *CHiPs*, a TV show that was popular in the early 1980s. In that episode, the two actors who portrayed police officers with the California Highway Patrol (or, more likely, the two stuntmen standing in for the actors) pulled their police car in front of a runaway car, slowed down to make contact with the front of the car, and kept slowing until it was stopped. The police officer thought the maneuver might work in real life. Fortunately, it did.

Teaching Tips:

For the reading: During the first reading of the story, you might pause at the point where the police officer arrives on the scene and asks students to speculate how the officer could help Ann stop her car. To prompt responses, suggest nonsensical scenarios, such as, "Do you think the officer says, 'Good luck!' and drives away?"

For the pronunciation exercise: Students might find it helpful to write the numbers in the air with their fingers as they say them. Students might also benefit from practicing the pronunciation of confusing pairs of numbers (13/30, 14/40, etc.).

For the speaking exercise: This is a TPR (Total Physical Response) activity. Please see the suggested steps under Teaching Tips in Unit 3.

For the writing exercise: Students who are confident writers may wish to cover the sentences with a piece of paper and write from memory, making the activity a dictation rather than a copying exercise.

Unit 10

AN EXPENSIVE VACATION

The two Canadian men, both 29 years old, were skiing at a resort in Montana when they decided to leave a marked trail and take a shortcut down to a lower trail. They ended up at the bottom of a ravine that was filled with waist-high snow. When they didn't return to their motel at 6:30 P.M., a search party of 40 rescuers was organized. After the skiers were found, the leader of the search-and-rescue group told the *Whitefish Pilot*, "The guys weren't in bad shape. They had warm clothing on, and they were doing what they should have been doing to stay warm."

Authorities say that Don and Jack's decision to burn the money probably saved their lives. They were skiing in January, when nighttime temperatures in the mountains are frigid; it can be as cold as −50 degrees Fahrenheit. If they had not been able to get a fire started, they might not have survived.

The men had the lighter with them because they had found it earlier that day on the slopes.

Teaching Tip:

As students share their completed sentences in the writing / speaking exercise, you may wish to write their responses on the board in a chart, for example:

Name	Where	What
Miriama	in her village	singing to the children
Alex	Prague	eating in a restaurant

You can then reinforce grammatical forms by asking questions based on the chart, for example: "Is Alex in his village?" ("No, he isn't. He's in Prague.") "Is Miriama eating in a restaurant?" ("No, she isn't. She's singing to the children.")

You may wish to tape the students' drawings around the room after students share their completed sentences. Then you can point to pictures and ask, for example, "Where is Alex?" ("He's in Prague.") "What's he doing?" ("He's eating in a restaurant.")

Unit 11

THE PARKING TICKET

The "police officer" was a traffic warden named Doris, who works in Petersfield, England. In the textbook version of the story, Colin parked next to the "NO PARKING" sign every day. Actually, his strategy was more subtle: He varied his parking violations. Later, Doris confessed that she had been suspicious. "He always seemed to be parked wherever I went," she told the *Mirror*. Colin said his plan was simply "trying to get myself noticed by her as often as possible by parking where I shouldn't."

Even after she suspected that Colin was parking illegally just to get her attention, Doris continued to give him tickets. After all, her nickname is "The Little Rottweiler" because she is one of the strictest traffic wardens in Petersfield. She warned that her new husband would not get preferential treatment. "He has to stick to the rules," she said. "He'll still get a ticket if he misbehaves."

Newspaper accounts do not divulge exactly how much Colin paid in parking fines all together, but one can assume it was a substantial sum. The fine for a single offense, £30, was equivalent to $60 at the time Colin was courting Doris.

Unit 12

THE PRESENT

The line of people who contributed to buy the toy was actually longer than the line in the story, and the present was more expensive. It was a Sega PlayStation 2, the only present the woman's son had asked for. She had saved all year to buy the gift, priced at $220. Some of the people in the long line at the WalMart in Cleburne, Texas, contributed $5, some $10, some a wad of singles. There was also a check for $50, made out to WalMart. It is not known if the woman ever found her money.

Unit 13

THE TAXI RIDE

Clifton's mother was busy unloading suitcases from her car at the John F. Kennedy Airport in New York when Clifton disappeared. The Associated Press, which reported Clifton's adventure, did not recount the exact sequence of events that led to the mix-up. A likely scenario is that the driver was standing outside the taxi, perhaps drinking a cup of coffee or talking to other drivers, when Clifton and the woman got in the taxi. The woman probably got into the taxi just seconds after Clifton.

The woman's destination was the Bronx, 20 miles from the airport, so Clifton's taxi ride lasted a good hour, round trip. When Clifton was reunited with his mother and two brothers, they continued on their journey to Haiti.

Teaching Tips:
For the pronunciation exercise: You might want to have students place their fingertips on their throats to feel the vibration when they make the sounds [z] and [ð] and note the lack of vibration when they make the sounds [s] and [Θ].

For the speaking exercise: This can be done as a chain activity. Sit in a circle with no more than 15 students. (Large classes will need to form several groups.) Begin the activity by stating what you like to do, for example, "I like to swim." Then, pointing to yourself, ask the student to your left, "What do I like to do?" The student (let's say his name is Koji) says, "You like to swim." Ask Koji, "What do *you* like to do?" Koji says, for example, "I like to watch movies." Pointing to yourself, ask the student next to Koji (let's say her name is Eva), "What do I like to do?" Eva says, "You like to swim." Point to Koji. Eva responds, "He likes to watch movies." Then ask Eva, "What do *you* like to do?" As you go around the circle, students first recite what the people before them like to do and then add their own statements. Of course, the last person in the circle has the most difficult task.

Unit 14

INTERNET FRIEND

Ken Walker thought he was having a stroke. As his vision began to blur, he had the impression that his keyboard was melting. "Helo," he wrote. "have problemd,,,,thhimk I am waying stroke. By keyboatd it melting." [*sic*] In his confused state, it never occurred to him to pick up the phone and call someone for help. Doctors at the hospital told him that he had probably suffered some sort of epileptic seizure, perhaps triggered by his flickering computer screen. He later told CNN during an interview, "I don't know what would have happened if paramedics hadn't turned up. All I remember is I thought I was going to die."

Ken had logged on to a genealogy Web site, where members chat live every Tuesday at 10 P.M. eastern time. Because of the time difference, Ken rarely participated in the discussion but often posted messages for people seeking help tracing their Scottish ancestry. This time, for a change, a member of the forum was able to help him.

Ken Walker lives in the town of Arbroath, near the city of Dundee on the North Sea. The name of the town was changed to Montrose for the story because it is more easily pronounced. Montrose is an actual town not far from Arbroath.

ABOUT THE AUTHOR

Sandra Heyer has taught English to adults, young adults, university students, and middle- and high-school students. She currently teaches adult learners in Whitewater, Wisconsin, in a community-based program she co-founded and coordinates.

The *True Stories* reading series evolved from materials she prepared for her students in an effort to provide them with readings that were both high-interest and comprehensible. She continues to develop and pilot new material for the series in her own classroom.

ACKNOWLEDGMENTS

I wish to thank . . .

- Pamela Haglund, reference librarian at the Flathead County (Montana) Library, who verified the story "An Expensive Vacation"
- John Gray at Big Mountain Resort in Montana, who contributed his recollection of the story of the two lost skiers
- Jorge Islas, Whitewater (Wisconsin) Community Education, who welcomed me into his classroom to field test stories and exercises
- Student artists Manuel Rivera and Awa Bakayoko, who provided the drawings for Units 1 and 10
- Dana Klinek at Longman, who skillfully guided this book through its middle stages, and Laura Lazzaretti, who skillfully guided it through its last
- Laura Le Dréan at Longman, first reader of all the *True Stories*
- John Heyer, first listener to all the *True Stories*

TEXT CREDITS

- The speaking activity in Units 1 and 10 is suggested by Sharron Bassano and Mary Ann Christison in *Drawing Out*, Alta Book Center Publishers, 1995.
- The speaking activity in Units 3, 5, and 9 is inspired by James Asher's *Total Physical Response Method*. These particular steps are recommended by Laurel Pollard and Natalie Hess in *Zero Prep*, Alta Book Center Publishers, 1997. ("Act It Out," p. 85)
- The singing activity in Units 7 and 11 is described by Laurel Pollard, Natalie Hess, and Jan Herron in *Zero Prep for Beginners*, Alta Book Center Publishers, 2001. ("Singing Dictation," p. 2)

PHOTO CREDITS

UNIT 1
Genesio's Gift
Courtesy of *Great Falls Tribune*

UNIT 2
The Surprise
© Ben Lack

UNIT 3
Hiccup! Hiccup!
© Corbis

UNIT 4
Wrong Number
The Columbus Dispatch

UNIT 5
The Catch
The Toronto Sun

UNIT 6
Fufu Returns
Don Tremain/Photodisc/Getty Images

UNIT 7
Not Too Small
AP/Wide World Photos

UNIT 8
Mario's Rabbits
AP/Wide World Photos

UNIT 9
No Brakes!
Helen Richardson, *Denver Post*

UNIT 10
An Expensive Vacation
© Index Stock Imagery, Inc.

UNIT 11
The Parking Ticket
Solent News and Photo Agency

UNIT 12
The Present
Brand X Pictures

UNIT 13
The Taxi Ride
Tony Fioranelli/Multi Media Network News

UNIT 14
Internet Friend
Ryan McVay/Photodisc/Getty Images

Answer Key

UNIT 1

Vocabulary
1. a car   2. in a house   3. clothes   4. money   5. to a concert

Comprehension
He...
☑ drives a small car.
☑ has a garden.
☑ wears old clothes.
☑ lives in a small house.
☑ goes to free concerts in the park.

Writing
1. Genesio is a custodian.   2. He cleans the classrooms at a university.   3. He makes money, but he doesn't like to spend it.   4. He dies when he is 102 years old.   5. He gives 2.3 million dollars to the university.

UNIT 2

Spelling
1. boyfriend   2. far   3. miss   4. tell   5. buy   6. plane

Vocabulary
1. plane ticket   2. Australia   3. far away   4. surprise
5. England

Comprehension
1. b   2. b   3. a   4. b   5. b   6. a

UNIT 3

Vocabulary
1. tongue   2. farmer   3. fingers   4. pull   5. lift   6. mouth

Comprehension
1. hiccup   2. glass   3. sugar   4. holds   5. swallows   6. 68
7. happy

UNIT 4

Vocabulary
1. wall   2. answer the phone   3. wrong number   4. shocked
5. crash   6. evening

Comprehension
1. b   2. b   3. a   4. b   5. a   6. a   7. a   8. a

Writing
Mary is tired. She goes into the living room and sits down in her favorite chair. The phone rings in the kitchen. A young woman asks, "Is this 555-4132?" Mary says, "You have the wrong number." A car hits Mary's house. The living room wall falls on Mary's chair. Mary is shocked.

UNIT 5

Spelling
1. nine   2. six   3. girl   4. look   5. boy   6. floor

Vocabulary
1. fourth floor   2. shoulder   3. blanket   4. hold   5. crawl
6. paramedic

Comprehension
1. e   2. c   3. a   4. g   5. f   6. d   7. b

UNIT 6

Spelling
1. happy   2. house   3. find   4. eight   5. year   6. day

Vocabulary
1. male   2. dish   3. leave   4. kitten   5. jump

Comprehension
1. b   2. b   3. b   4. a   5. b   6. a

UNIT 7

Spelling
1. school   2. play   3. practice   4. boys   5. small   6. walk

Vocabulary
1. lake   2. road   3. football   4. pull   5. weights   6. laugh

Comprehension
1. Justin   2. the car   3. the boys   4. the man   5. Justin
6. the man   7. the car   8. the boys

UNIT 8

Spelling
1. want   2. doesn't   3. know   4. buy   5. other   6. people
7. house   8. only

Vocabulary
1. male   2. female   3. sofa   4. keeps   5. month   6. pet

Comprehension
1. rabbit   2. two   3. likes   4. 73   5. house   6. take   7. one rabbit

UNIT 9

Spelling
80 eighty;   50 fifty;   30 thirty;   40 forty;   20 twenty;
90 ninety;   70 seventy;   10 ten;   100 one hundred;
60 sixty

Vocabulary
1. highway   2. pass   3. brake   4. kick   5. hug   6. accelerator

Comprehension
1. b   2. c   3. e   4. a   5. d

UNIT 10

Vocabulary
1. mountain   2. lost   3. fire   4. wood   5. bills   6. expensive

Comprehension

1. ~~swimming~~; skiing **2.** ~~lunch~~; fire **3.** ~~paper~~; money **4.** ~~spend~~; burn **5.** ~~afternoon~~; night **6.** ~~sad~~; fine

UNIT 11

Vocabulary

1. smile **2.** expensive **3.** a parking ticket **4.** marry **5.** sign **6.** a lot of parking tickets

Comprehension

1. next to **2.** police officer **3.** ticket **4.** lot **5.** see (or talk to) **6.** later

UNIT 12

Vocabulary

1. toys **2.** line **3.** holiday **4.** wallet **5.** present **6.** pass

Comprehension

1. a **2.** a **3.** b **4.** b **5.** a **6.** a

Writing

It is December 24, the day before a big holiday. People are buying presents. Mrs. Park is holding a toy. It is a present for her son. Her money is gone. The people in line pay for the toy.

UNIT 13

Vocabulary

1. c **2.** e **3.** a **4.** f **5.** b **6.** d

Comprehension

1. b **2.** b **3.** b **4.** a **5.** a **6.** b **7.** a

UNIT 14

Vocabulary

1. d **2.** f **3.** a **4.** e **5.** b **6.** c

Comprehension

1. a **2.** b **3.** b **4.** a **5.** b **6.** b **7.** a **8.** a

Writing

It is 3 A.M. in Scotland. Ken Walker has a bad headache. He wants to "talk" to people on the Internet. Suddenly Ken feels very, very sick. He types, "Have problem. Need help." The man in the United States calls an operator in Scotland. The police take Ken to the hospital. Doctors give him medicine, and he is OK.

Your Own Paper